REMEMBERING
THE TIME

THE REANIMATION OF GOD'S PEOPLE
AND LIVING AND SHARING
THE GOOD NEWS

George Providence II

NARROWGate
PUBLISHING

REMEMBERING THE TIME:
THE REANIMATION OF GOD'S PEOPLE AND LIVING
AND SHARING THE GOOD NEWS
By George Providence II
Copyright © 2024 George Providence II
ISBN: 979-8-218-55249-7

Thanks to Priscilla Du Preez on Unsplash for photo.

NARROWGate
PUBLISHING

To my wife, Lynn, the bringer of fire and my love and partner for life; to my daughters, Brittany and Tiffany—they have been my most consistent earthly joy; and to my mother, Barbara Ann Providence, whose passing earlier this year has intensified my hunger for heaven. She was, quite simply, the greatest woman I have ever known.

TABLE OF CONTENTS

Acknowledgments

There are countless individuals that I would like to thank for their influence in my life and who, in their way, had a hand in the writing of this book. I would like to thank the following, but will no doubt miss some important names. Please charge it to my head, not my heart:

The late Reverend James C. Offutt Sr. It was in watching him that I realized what a true man of Christ looked like.

The late Dr. Steven Moore and Dennis Polkow, the advisors during my time as editor of the student newspapers at Chicago State University and Oakton Community College, respectively. Their sharp tongues and insightful minds pushed me to be a better thinker.

Pastor Keith A. King, Christian Tabernacle Church. A kindred spirit with respect to our approaches to ministry, he gave me permission to work through much of the content of *Remembering the Time* as a member of Christian Tabernacle Baptist Church.

Reverend Deborah Newton, my running buddy while at Christian Tab, who always had me cracking up and kept me encouraged. Pastor Jeff Murriel, for taking the time to read the book in its raw form and offering up valuable reflections.

My sister Michelle Shelfer, a godsend whose gentle, kind spirit and editorial expertise smoothed out the many rough edges of *Remembering the Time*.

And finally, I want to thank my three most important earthly influences. My late mother, Barbara Providence. She always believed in me, always encouraged me, and never stopped loving me. My wife, Lynn Providence, the ball of fire who has taken the baton from my mother and does not let me forget that through Christ, all things are possible. My late father, George Sr., known as "Bag o' Brains" in his home country, whose creativity and talent for dreaming the improbable continue to inspire me today.

Note to the Reader

This book was written with an eye toward fostering both reflection for the individual and discussion for group Bible study, and the questions at the end of the chapters are meant to provoke both. If *Remembering the Time* is used for a group Bible study or a workshop, the author recommends triads, or groups of three, for reflection and discussion.

George Providence II, with his wife, Lynn, is the proud parent of seven mostly grown children and—at the time of this writing—six grandchildren. He has pastored and preached for over thirty years and is the founder of NARROWGate Ministries,[1] dedicated to working with individuals seeking to make it to the narrow door. He is also featured on that ministry's podcast, *A Quick Word*.

---

1. Go to narrowgate-ministries.com.

George and Lynn, a licensed counselor, lead the workshop series, Exploring the Covenant, focused on married couples and singles contemplating marriage.

We should not ask, "What is wrong with the world?" for that diagnosis has already been given. Rather, we should ask, "What has happened to the salt and light?"

—John R. W. Stott

The Most Sacred Task: Telling Others the Good News

Then the Spirit said to Philip, "Go near
and overtake this chariot." So Philip
ran to him, and heard him reading the
prophet Isaiah, and said, "Do you understand what you are reading?" And he said,
"How can I, unless someone guides me?"
And he asked Philip to come up and sit
with him. (Acts 8:29–31)

Time to tell the truth and shame the devil—the first two times I entered a church of my own volition, I was chasing skirts. I was fourteen, and one of my best friends growing up was a boy named Willie Eaton. Willie had freckles, his daddy was a preacher or deacon as I recall, and he had a sister named Michelle, whose dark beauty and preternatural curves expanded the boundaries of my adolescent imagination.

Willie and I hung pretty tight, and we enjoyed each other's company, playing pickup games of whatever sport was in season, but it was Michelle that I was always trying to get a glimpse of when I went by his apartment. Michelle had my nose wide open, but she paid me no mind. One day out of the blue, Willie invited me to his family's church. I did not go to church—ever—because I thought that most of the guys that I knew who went to church were jelly-backed, but I instantly recognized the opportunity. Michelle was going to have to give me some time. How could she ignore me in the Lord's house? Well, somehow, she managed. Outside of a grunt and grimace of acknowledgment that I was indeed in her presence—and that provoked by vigorous prompting by her mother—Michelle bade me not a moment's more consideration. The sermon I heard that Sunday morning, "Time Is Winding Up!" with its urgent message of self-examination in light of the imminent return of Christ (or the demise of the hearer), has stayed with me even until now, forty years later.

It would be another three years before I darkened the threshold of a church again.

This time, it was a girl named Bernadette Alston. She was a year older than I was, an aspiring model (a model!) and very assertive. Unlike Michelle, Bernadette had a definite interest in your boy, but she made it abundantly clear that to get to the promised land, I would need to show up at church with her and her family. She did not have to ask me twice!

Now, with over twenty-five years in the ministry, I have indeed found superior motivations for showing up on a Sunday morning. Still, I mention these first two experiences because they highlight something that I think is critically important concerning evangelism. Those first two times I was in church, I got there because of somebody that I knew. Willie and I were friends. Bernadette and I were playing at being boyfriend and girlfriend. I was exposed to the Gospel of Jesus Christ because of those relationships. It has been my experience that this is the case for most Christians. When we first came to Christ—when we first showed up to a church on our own—it was because we knew somebody who was already there. Most of us experienced the Lord at work as someone we knew allowed Christ to manifest Himself in them. More importantly, that someone we knew had an authentic relationship with Jesus Christ, and we wanted the same thing for ourselves.

I have written this book to Christians as a way of changing their evangelistic purview. I believe that our relationships, specifically our relationship with the Lord and our relationship with others, are vital in the communication of the Gospel of Jesus Christ. I also believe that the transmission of the Gospel of Jesus Christ is the Christian's most sacred duty.

Relationship is personal, and it is often intimate. Evangelism, the sharing of the good news of Jesus Christ, is also personal—also often intimate. And relationship and the sharing of the Gospel always involve you and someone else. For me, that someone else could be my children, my siblings, my parents, or my grandchildren. These are my loved ones, and when I think of evangelism and how important it is, I think of them. But these are not my only relationships. I also think about my coworkers and friends, both past and present. I also wonder about those that I dislike or who dislike me, for, though these can be difficult and distasteful, they are relationships nonetheless.

When I think of evangelism, I think of people. Evangelism is a deeply personal thing to me. It involves the people that I care about the most but also includes those that I care about the least. All are the object of the Lord's affection and are the beneficiaries of His gift of eternal life. Christians often think of evangelism as the thing that is done "out there." It is that thing that we do outside of the church to people we do not know and who do not know us—and yes, there is some truth to this. Mark 16:15 (ESV) tells Christians to "Go into all the world and proclaim the Gospel," and yes, this we should do, but this should not be the entirety of our effort. Those that are near us—in our home, our school, our place of employ, and our church—also need to hear (and see) the Gospel.

I came to the Lord through the relationship I developed with a pastor, Alphra Love. I had just left a church that I had been a member of for two years. When I first joined the church, it was to sing in the choir—nothing more. I attended Sunday services but never Sunday school. I did not pray. I did not read more than a page of the Bible. I sang about Him but did not know Him, and the dissonance began to wear on me. I wanted to live with integrity and became uncomfortable because I did not. That discomfort pushed me out of that church, but I left it determined that I would make one final attempt at the Bible to get some under-standing—or be done with the whole thing. It was at this point that Pastor Love came into my life.

She gave me her number and told me that I could call her at any time with questions that I had concerning Scripture. She directed me to the book of Mark. I purchased a version of the Bible I'd seen advertised on TV by Capt. Kirk (I'm a *Star Trek* guy) called The Book, and for two weeks I called Pastor Love. We talked for hours as she patiently answered every question I had until it came to that most important one: Would I accept Christ as my Savior? With a genuine and surprising sense of awe and wonder, I answered yes.

After accepting the gift of salvation, answering the call to the ministry, and serving in Pastor Love's Pentecostal Assemblies of the World Church for two years, I entered full-time ministry at a Mennonite/Church of the Brethren congregation in Evanston, Illinois.

The church was situated in a diverse but mostly African-American low-income neighborhood. The outliers in the community were the members of Reba Place Church and Fellowship—a church initially established as an intentional Christian community. The model for the church was the community of believers described in Acts 4. The composition of their church was mostly white, with a few notable exceptions. The members of the church, in addition to worshiping in the community, also lived there. They stood, by choice, as a bulwark against the ravages of white flight that occurred when black folks began to move into the neighborhood.

After a time, the members of Reba Place Church began to feel the incongruity of a mostly white congregation in a now-primarily black neighborhood. That felt incongruity moved them to seek out African-American leadership to show them the way to reach out to the community to act, as it were, as a bridge between their African-American neighbors and themselves. Reverend James C. Offutt Sr., a Baptist pastor from central Illinois who had a long history of cross-racial ministry, was that bridge. I had the privilege of being mentored by him, and after two years, I became the associate pastor for evangelism and outreach for the church.

My primary task was to create a context for bringing those who knew Christ—those inside the church—together with those who did not know Christ and were outside of the church. During my almost nine years as a member first of the laity and then as full-time staff, I learned a few things. I learned that it is deceptively easy to bring church folks and unchurched folks together. Free food and childcare—free anything for that matter—will pull them together every time. Believe it.

However, bringing them together was not the same thing as keeping them together—let alone getting them to worship together. I learned that despite the years that they had professed Christ, many Christians were often anxious about what to say about Christ when speaking to the unsaved. I also learned that the manner in which one did ministry—indeed, the manner in which one lived one's life—mattered much to those who received the words that followed. In effect, actions validated words. I learned that people often agreed that change needed to happen, but they did not necessarily agree that *they* needed to change. And I learned that the most effective way to present Jesus was always out of relationship. If there was no relationship, there was little if any opportunity to gain a reasonable hearing for the good news. But when I knew the person and that person knew me, Jesus could be introduced with more ease.

So, I began to develop strategies and programs to facilitate the creation of relationships between those in the church and those outside the church. I saw what happened when good, God-fearing, God-loving people, seeking to present the good news, allowed those they were in a relationship with to witness them living with transparent abandon for the Lord. Through good times and bad, unbelievers vicariously experienced Christ through the lives of the members of Reba Place Church, and many of them began to hunger for Jesus. When we made it a priority to be in and of the community—to be in a relationship with the community—said community sampled what it was like to be part of an authentic Christian experience. They did not see perfection, but they saw the process of being made perfect. And people came to Reba Place Church because they wanted that experience for themselves. Conversely, I also learned that the hunger for Jesus could dissipate when Christians chose to live less authentically, less auspiciously, and less ostentatiously for Christ.

I am both honored and humbled by this opportunity to share with you what I have gleaned over the years concerning the joyous work of evangelism. And yes, it is a joy. It is a joy to share with others how the good news has changed me—remade me. It is a joy to tell someone who has possibly given up on life—whose humble aspirations have gone for naught, who despairs the coming sunrise or dreads the impending sunset—that hope yet lives. There is reason to look expectantly toward the breaking of a new dawn. Despite your circumstance, despite the shroud of depravity that darkens all that you see, there is another way. You can be forgiven. You can be free—free of the shackles of self-hatred and recrimination. Free from the bondage of fear and trepidation concerning what the future may bring, whether that future is next year, next week, or the next minute. You can be free of the rage and frustration that roil your insides and threaten to boil over at the merest of provocations. For those so bound—so caught up—Jesus extends that most perplexing and yet exhilarating of invitations: "Come to Me, all you who labor and are heavy laden, and I will give you rest. Take My yoke upon you and learn from Me, for I am gentle and lowly in heart, and you will find rest for your souls. For My yoke is easy and My burden is light" (Matthew 11:28–30).

Those who have given themselves to Jesus Christ can testify: true freedom from bondage is found in enslavement to Him.

We champion freedom here in the United States. This nation was born out of a desire for freedom. We have fought wars to both protect and secure freedom. We proudly proclaim that we are the land of the free. Freedom is our most cherished possession. However, it is the exercise of that freedom unmoored from Christ that betrays the need for that selfsame Christ. A survey of the headlines on any given day provides a tragic illustration of this truth.

At the time of this writing, a man has posted a video of himself holding the severed head of his father while declaring himself the acting president of the United States. He says his father was a traitor to his country.[1]

A famous popstar's face is digitally superimposed on a body engaged in pornographic activities. The opinion writer reporting on this believes that "our humanity is a click away from being used against us."[2]

A husband divorces after one month of marriage when his twenty-four-year-old wife, a teacher, is

---

1. Melissa Alonso et al., "Man Arrested after Video Post Showed Severed Head of His Father, Police Say, amid Political Rant that Stayed Online for Hours," CNN, February 1, 2024, cnn.com/2024/01/31/us/justin-mohn-father-beheaded-biden-video/index.html.

2. Laurie Segall, "The Taylor Swift AI Photos Offer a Terrifying Warning," CNN *Opinion*, January 31, 2024, cnn.com/2024/01/31/opinions/taylor-swift-deepfakes-ai-segall/index.html.

convicted of committing "lascivious acts" with boys aged twelve and thirteen. She faces thirty-three years in prison.[3]

I do not mean to say that there are no bright spots against this dark backdrop of confusion, pain, misanthropy, and despair, but oh, how this world needs a Savior! How this world needs Christ! How this world needs the Lord! And this world needs a people willing to submit themselves to His will, His way!

It is my prayer that you are among those people willing to give of yourself as He gave Himself for you. I pray that those you interact with—be they family, friend, or foe—will see in you a good and vivid example of the efficacy of Jesus Christ and His ability to transform the lives of those that are willing to allow Him into their lives. Our time is still in need of saving—still in need of believing. But before our world can believe, those of us who are called by His name must be willing to hear His voice and to follow. We must be ready to be

---

3. Yaron Steinbuch, "Newlywed Iowa Teacher Admits Sex Abuse of Boys as Young as 13," *New York Post*, February 1, 2024, nypost.com/2024/02/01/news/former-iowa-teacher-pleads-guilty-to-having-sex-with-teens-shortly-after-marriage/.

the Lord's living testimonies—walking, breathing advertisements of the new world available to them if they would but believe.

The living and sharing of the good news, the Gospel, is what we will explore. We will spend some time discussing the definition, the process, and the *why* of evangelism. It is my hope that you and I will come to a common understanding about evangelism. I also hope that you can see how we, through word and deed, can help our families, friends, coworkers, and communities imagine for themselves new possibilities found only in Christ.

By "the reanimation of God's people," I do not mean that we are dead—that I am a modern-day Ezekiel, speaking to a valley of dry bones. Instead, by reanimation, I am speaking to the need for Christians to regain the vim and vigor, the contagious excitement in the sharing of the Gospel that we once (hopefully) had. It is good news, after all, and should be an uplift for us and for our hearers.

Remembering the Time speaks to the necessity of Christians to recover the memory of their identity in Christ. Too many of us live as if we have never encountered the risen Savior. For many of us, the passion—the fire that was shut up in our bones immediately following our salvation—has cooled considerably. For many now, with the passage of time, there is little in our day-to-day living that would differentiate the professor of Christ from one who scarcely pays Him any attention at all. We no longer wonder, as the gospel great Mahalia Jackson sang, how we got over. We must remember who we are if we are to be effective in evangelism.

With Facebook, YouTube, Instagram, Twitter, Netflix, Hulu, Amazon Prime, and on-demand TV, it is easy to become distracted from the necessity of tending to one's inner self. Self-examination, though, is a must if we expect to reach out to others with the good news of Jesus Christ. Is it reasonable to assume that you will speak of the things of God to those outside of the faith if you are unwilling to examine the interior of your own heart? Singer Teddy Pendergrass told the truth when he said that you "can't hide from yourself." Truth be told, we really can't hide from those that we interact with on a regular basis. Don't get it twisted—your kids know who you are. Your spouse knows who you are. Your siblings, your parents, your friends—they all can see behind the veil. We do all that we can to drown out that still, small voice telling us—pleading with us—to move and govern ourselves in a certain way. Sadly, we do not want to hear the voice of Christ, for it may well mean that there are severe changes in our lives that must be made—changes that, in truth, we are loath to make. Yet, it is precisely this kind of honesty that we must have if we are to witness to others about the mercy and love of Jesus Christ.

Know that I do not speak as one who looks down from on high and judges. Instead, I speak as one who labors to stay on the straight and narrow path—one who, upon reflection, is sometimes overwhelmed with shame at the corrupt nature of my thoughts and actions. I journey along the same steep path as do you, seeking entrance through the narrow gate to life. What we will explore together in the pages to follow should be challenging, but my prayer is that together, with the Lord's help, we will accelerate you along the path on which the Lord is already leading you.

Let us begin.

For reflection:

1. Do you remember when you made the choice to come to Christ? Was there an event that moved you, or was there someone who helped guide you to Him?

2. Whom do you think of when you think of sharing the Gospel?

3. Can you imagine sharing the Gospel with a neighbor? A colleague? An adversary or enemy?

Chapter One

The goal of Christian mission is not success, but faithful witness; not power, but proclamation; not technique, but truth; not method, but message.

—Michael Horton

REDUCE TO THE IRREDUCIBLE:
CLARIFYING THE MISSION

But He said to them, "I must preach the
kingdom of God to the other cities also,
because for this purpose I have been sent."
(Luke 4:43)

As a good friend of mine used to say, under-standing is a beautiful thing. Toward that end, I want us to come to a mutual understanding of the terms *evangelism*, *Gospel*, and *mission*.

A simple search of the internet will return Wikipedia's definition of *evangelism*, which says that it is "the act of preaching the Gospel."[1] The website for 3Ps Christian Ministries states that "evangelism is the announcement, proclamation,

---

1. Wikipedia; Wikipedia's "Evangelism" entry, accessed January 16, 2024.

and/or preaching of the Gospel, the good news of and about Jesus Christ."[2] Further, 3Ps goes on to say that "the Gospel is a communicated message, communicated in verbal and/or written form." Another definition, found in the *Dictionary of Bible Themes*, says that *evangelism* is "the proclamation of the good news of Jesus Christ, which arises naturally from the believers' love for God and appreciation of all that God has done for them."[3] Personally, I like this definition, but it still is missing something.

The above definitions are all satisfactory, yet, as useful as they are, each omits an essential element: the reconciliation of one's words with one's behavior. There is a necessity of the proclaimer of the good news to live the good news. This cannot be overstated. There is an inextricable link between our walk and our proclamation. We Christians must walk it like we talk it. The preaching of the Gospel, sharing the good news, cannot be a do-as-I-say-but-not-as-I-do affair. You may demur, but for

---

2. "The Need for Evangelism," 3Ps Christian Ministries, September 8, 2014, accessed January 30, 2024, 3psministries.org/sermons/the-need-for-evangelism/.

3. *Dictionary of Bible Themes*, s.v. "evangelism (*n.*)," accessed January 16, 2024, biblegateway.com/resources/dictionary-of-bible-themes/8424-evangelism.

the purposes of our discussion, let us agree that the definition of *evangelism* will be the preaching *and the living* of the Christian Gospel. As James 1:22 says, we are to "be doers of the word, and not hearers only." Evangelism is the announcement, proclamation, and/or preaching of the Gospel and the living out of the Gospel of and about Jesus Christ. Evangelism happens when we both declare the good news of Jesus Christ and provide an actual demonstration of that good news working itself out in our lives. Evangelism arises naturally from the believers' love for God and appreciation of all that God has done for them and the desire to share that good news with someone else.

Dictionary.com has many definitions of the word *Gospel*, such as "the teachings of Jesus and the apostles," "the story of Christ's life and teachings," and any one of the four books penned by Matthew, Mark, Luke, or John as proper understandings of the word. But I settled upon the sixth entry provided. It says that the *Gospel* is "glad tidings, especially concerning salvation and the kingdom of God as announced to the world by Christ."[4] The

---

4. Dictionary.com, s.v. "Gospel" (*n.*), accessed January 16, 2024, dictionary.com/browse/gospel.

Dictionary of Bible Themes agrees, stating that the *Gospel* is "the good news of God's redemption of sinful humanity through the life, death, and resurrection of His Son Jesus Christ."[5] Perhaps nothing defines the meaning of the Gospel better than the words of Jesus Himself as He sat in the synagogue and in the hearing of all present: "The Spirit of the LORD is upon Me, …to preach the gospel to the poor; …to heal the brokenhearted, to proclaim liberty to the captives…, to proclaim the acceptable year of the LORD" (Luke 4:18–19). The Gospel—the good news—for the world is that the kingdom of God, in Christ, has arrived. The good news is that Christ has come to free the world from the consequences of sin. In Him, the forgiveness of sins, freedom from sin's bondage, and the hope of eternal life are found in the death, burial, and subsequent resurrection of Jesus Christ.

Merriam-Webster says that one definition of the word *mission* is "a specific task with which a person

---

5. *Dictionary of Bible Themes*, s.v. "Gospel (*n.*)," accessed January 16, 2024, biblegateway.com/resources/dictionary-of-bible-themes/2420-gospel.

or a group is charged,"[6] and this works very nicely when we think of the church as the group charged with a specific task. The question is, what is that task, what is that mission, and who has tasked us with this assignment?

The four Gospels give the reader four distinct pictures of the life of Jesus Christ during His sojourn here on earth. The authors, Matthew, Mark, Luke, and John, are storytellers, and they tell the story of Jesus's time on earth, His walk, and His ministry. Each Gospel writer shares the story of the work of Jesus on the earth as he saw it. They give us the events, tales, and tidbits that are most meaningful to them. Matthew, the tax collector, shares the story of Joseph and Mary being warned by an angel of the Lord to flee, for Herod is coming to kill Jesus. Mark recounts Jesus's words about the sowing of seed and the consequences when that seed lands on stony ground, amongst the thorns, or on good ground. The faithful physician, Luke, retells the compelling tale of the son who rejects his father and leaves home to live *la vida loca*, only to return

---

6. *Merriam-Webster Dictionary*, s.v. "mission (*n.*)," accessed January 16, 2024, merriam-webster.com/dictionary/mission.

humbled. And upon his return, he discovers that his father never gave up on him. John, the disciple whom Jesus loved, tells the reader that in the beginning was the Word, and the Word was with God, and the Word was God. Their individual accounts of the life and times of Jesus Christ differ in points of emphasis, yes, but they all come into harmony on the thrust of His last words. In one form or another, the Gospels all point to Jesus's command that His followers are to go into the world, preaching the Gospel and making disciples.

Last things said—those final instructions—are essential things. In the mind of the speaker, the last words said are details that must be attended to. Think for a moment and recall the final directions you received from your parents the first time they left you home alone. Recall, if you will, the scene in any war movie where the battle is in the offing. The soldier and spouse cling to each other for what may be the last time. The ensuing conversation is direct. It is earnest. It is intense. Rehearse in your mind the well-worn scene of a murder mystery where the victim uses their last moments to issue forth a dying declaration. The words they speak concerning the circumstances of their demise have tremendous weight.

All of these examples point to the importance of the last things shared by our Lord to the disciples. Go into the world and preach the Gospel. Make disciples. If they were to do nothing else, this would suffice. Because we, too, are disciples, this is our task—our mission. The spreading of the Gospel—the good news—was the most important thing that our Lord and Savior did while on earth. Indeed, I believe that it is the sum of His ministry—His mission—and is instructive for those of us who consider ourselves His followers. Let me sneak in one more term for us to get to a common understanding.

Both *Mounce's Complete Expository Dictionary of Old and New Testament Words* and the *New International Encyclopedia of Bible Words* have lengthy entries on the term *to follow*. In the Old Testament, the verb *to follow* often references a believer's demonstration of faith by hewing closely to the ways of God, His laws, statutes, and decrees. The Hebrew "walks after," or follows God and in so doing makes an active choice to reject the ways of the people around him and those he encounters. Rather than worship gods forged from fire or carved from wood, he will worship no other gods before the one true God. To be obedient to Yahweh is to refuse to engage in the abominable behavior of the worshippers of Molech or Chemosh. Choosing His way means not integrating the ways of the proselytes of Asherah or Ashtoreth into his lifestyle.

In the New Testament, *to follow* can have a common, descriptive meaning, but it also has special significance related to discipleship. Those who choose Christ choose to *follow* Him—to imitate His example. Zeus or Diana and the disciplines of their devotees were of no concern to those who embraced the Way, the Truth, and the Life.

Now, Jesus did much in His three and a half years of ministry. Healings, feedings, exorcisms, and resurrections—but I submit to you that all was done with an eye toward two overarching goals: preaching the good news and making disciples. And His expectation was that those who followed Him would do as He did.

The invitation to the fisherman casting nets into the sea was to follow Him and He would make them fishers of men (Matthew 4). And as noted before, His last instructions to His disciples before ascending to be with His Father was for His followers to go into all the world and preach the Gospel to every living creature (Mark 16:15). Matthew 28:18–19 delineates the task of the follower further, for, in addition to preaching the Gospel, Jesus's followers are to "make disciples"—believers who will follow the followers in the imitation of Christ. Following, though, can be difficult for the child of God.

After having lived in Philadelphia, New York City, Chicago, and Evanston, Illinois, for over thirty years, I decided to return home. I missed my mother and father and brothers. I had left New Haven as a cocky and egotistical nineteen-year-old boy, one who described himself as an agnostic on the subjects of God and the necessity of salvation to escape the tortures of hell. I returned a grandfather and ordained minister in search of a church home.

That search went on for close to five years as I auditioned, unsuccessfully, church after church after church. Make no mistake—much of my wandering had to do with my own peripatetic nature and what was wrong on the inside of me. Still, I usually found the Sunday-morning experience at our local churches unpalatable, mainly because most of the sermons I heard preached were, at the core, egocentric. The message for the most part was that God was a way-maker who makes a way, so that "I" could be blessed—so that "I" could move through the vicissitudes of life successfully. He made a way so that "I" could experience the totality of "me." Why? So that "I" could live in abundance, so that "I" could be the best "me" that "I" could be. Even messages that could be nominally referred to as bibliocentric seemed to fall short of the mark, for those messages often failed to point to the mission of Christ.

I believe that the incessant focus on "me" and "I" in our churches has demoted God's mission. We have sidelined His mission in pursuit of "our ministry," "our gifts," and "our calling," and once we are in possession and control of "our gifts," it makes it difficult—if not nigh impossible—to attend to *His mission*. Consumed with the relentless pursuit of our personal journeys—obsessed with gaining possession of that idiosyncratic, peculiar something that God has for us and only us—we lose sight of the true meaning of Jesus's sacrifice and the reality that we are but clay in the hands of the Potter, to be fashioned in service of His purpose. That we live is Christ, and to die is gain! You and I, we who have confessed Christ, have been bought for a price, and our lives are no longer our own.

Think it through. At work, you hold a position. You have a job and are assigned tasks. You are paid to perform those particular tasks. Now, you may well like these tasks. You may even feel a tremendous sense of fulfillment and ownership of the assigned tasks, but don't get it twisted. The job you have been assigned and paid to do must be performed in a way that is consistent with the overall mission of the company. You must complete the tasks given to you in a way that dovetails with the entity that has hired you. The company pays you to perform as instructed. Put another way, you have been bought for a price and are expected to work as directed.

Jesus Christ shed His blood for you and me, and in return, His mission is our mission. Each of us may, in the furtherance of Christ's mission, perform different tasks, but all of "our gifts," "our callings," and "our ministries" work explicitly to further the one mission.

Yes, there is much activity in the church. There is much work to do. Sermons, prayer meetings, Bible study, trustee meetings, deacon board meetings, youth group, choir, prison ministry, the feeding of the homeless—the list goes on and on. All of these activities are good such as they are, but sometimes—dare I say frequently—they become an end in themselves. I have become convinced that to the extent that this is true, we have missed our mark. This missing of the mark is exacerbated by the incessant search for an individual calling, a place to work "my gifts," the fulfillment of "my ministry." Our pursuit of self-actualization keeps our eyes on ourselves and what we want to achieve versus attending to the first and last things that Jesus said—the first an invitation "Come, follow" and the second the command to go into the world and preach the Gospel and make disciples. That is the end game—the propagation of the Gospel of Jesus Christ. All that we do should reflect that reality.

For reflection:

1. Do you agree or disagree with the statement that evangelism is not just one of the missions of the church, but it is *the* mission of the church?

2. If you agree with the statement, imagine that your life is a tabula rasa, a clean slate, and that you can construct your life in any manner you choose. How would you build your life today in the service of evangelism?

3. If you disagree with the statement, why? What do you see as more important?

God forbid that I should travel with any-body a quarter of an hour without speaking of Christ to them.

—George Whitfield

RESTORE TO ME THE JOY:
REMEMBERING THE TIME

Nevertheless I have this against you, that
you have left your first love. Remember
therefore from where you have fallen;
repent and do the first works, or else I
will come to you quickly and remove your
lampstand from its place—unless you
repent. (Revelation 2:4–5)

L et me paraphrase the words of a famous "poet"
of the twentieth century.

Do you remember when we fell in love?
We were young and innocent then.
Do you remember how it all began?
It just seemed like heaven.
So, why did it end?...
Back in the fall,

We'd be together
All day long…holding hands,
In each other's eyes we'd stare,
Tell me,
Do you remember the time when we fell in
love…
The time when we first met?…
When we fell in love?
Do you remember the time?
Do you remember how we used to talk?
We'd stay on the phone at night till dawn.
Do you remember all the things we said,
like,
"I love you so," and "I'll never let you go"?
Do you remember back in the spring?
Every morning birds would sing.
Do you remember those special times?
They'll just go on and on in the back of my
mind.
Do you remember the time?[1]

It happens, does it not? That blush of first love,
hot though it burns, turns cool—sometimes cold.

---

1. Michael Jackson, Teddy Riley, Bernard Belle,
"Remember the Time," 1992, from *Dangerous*, Epic
Records, New York.

As B. B. King sang, "The thrill is gone." We do lose that loving feeling. The honeymoon is over. It seems that this is the way of all things—all relationships. What once was red hot is now cool, if not ice cold.

It is proverbial: we can give only that which we already possess. The Gospel is no exception. If we want others to be excited about the Gospel, we, too, must be excited. We were excited once upon a time. Back when we first accepted Christ—back when the new life in Him was a marvel to behold—we burned for Him, yearned for more of Him. Fresh were the memories of our captive, bound lives, and we praised Him for saving us. Until one day, the fire died.

This is not a new phenomenon. The exile of Patmos, John the apostle, transcribed these words at the instruction of Christ for the church of Ephesus: "Nevertheless I have this against you, that you have left your first love (Revelation 2:4).

As profoundly as we may love Him, as strong as our commitment to Him may be, somehow, we have lost some of the passion that we had when we first came to Christ. He is real but not as immediate. He is ever-present yet not always felt. He has helped us overcome, but we've not necessarily needed Him to maintain. It is so easy to fall into the habit of taking care of what we can take care of and leaving to the Lord that which is beyond our means. In the process, we subvert the invitation to carry all concerns to Him. He is no longer essential to the living of our day-to-day.

What happened? In Revelation 2:4, Jesus says the church of Ephesus has left Him. He is no longer their first love. Despite being a church that labored in His name—a church that was patient and did not countenance evil—despite having persevered for His name's sake and refusing to quit, Jesus is no longer the center of their joy. One commentator observes that "loving devotion to Christ can be lost in the midst of active service." In Mark 4:18–19, Jesus asserts that we may let the cares of the world take a front seat in our lives. We allow ourselves to believe the lie that having a fat stack of Benjamins will make everything alright, or, quite simply, we adopt the attitude of the world and pursue our desires regardless of whether or not those desires square with our profession of faith. The Savior and Lord of our lives and His mission take a backseat.

Like most, there was a particular period in my life when I was on fire for the Lord. That Jesus should be glorified was my sole aim. I traveled to Zimbabwe on a mission trip to feed a village that suffered under the debilitating effects of famine. While there, I preached, and as a result, I saw dozens of school kids and young adults come to Christ. I returned home and preached at a midnight basketball league organized by the City of Chicago as a way of keeping African-American young men from shooting each other in the middle of the night. Street-hardened young gangsters became pliable under the administration of the Word and gave their lives to the Lord. During one Thanksgiving week, the Lord brought into my life three women who claimed to be on the verge of suicide, and through His power, they chose life over death. Parents would bring their children or significant others to me so that together, we could seek the Lord. Through it all, I felt as if I was in consort with the weeping prophet, Jeremiah, who said that "His Word was in my heart like a burning fire shut up in my bones."[2]

And then, one day, it was gone. That fire that I had felt left, quenched by busyness. Yes, I was tremendously busy—there were few who were more active—but in my rush to do the work of the church, I neglected my pursuit of the Lord. Good

---

2. Jeremiah 20:9.

work, yes, but the work had become an end in itself. I had forsaken my first love.

Does that sound familiar? As you reflect upon the rhythm of your day-to-day life, is Christ ascendant? Yes? Then, no worries. But if He does not reign supreme within you, how can you expect others to make Him their priority?

We must return to our first love. For me, I find a particular peace in the words of David in the fifty-first psalm. When I contemplate my witness and how I've fallen short, it is these words that reignite my fire:

> Create in me a clean heart, O God; and renew a right spirit within me.
>
> Cast me not away from Thy presence; and take not Thy Holy Spirit from me.
>
> Restore unto me the joy of Thy salvation; and uphold me with Thy free spirit.
>
> Then will I teach transgressors Thy ways; and sinners shall be converted unto Thee.
>
> Deliver me from bloodguiltiness, O God, Thou God of my salvation: and my tongue shall sing aloud of Thy righteousness.

O Lord, open Thou my lips; and my mouth
shall shew forth Thy praise.
(Psalm 51:10–15 KJV)

Do you want to know what to say when talking
to those who do not know Jesus Christ? Present
yourself to the Lord and allow Him to search out
your heart. Give Him permission to renew your
spirit by His Spirit, and He will restore the joy of
your salvation. Then will your tongue float with the
words of life—the good news that the kingdom of
God is here and that those once condemned can
be free. Present yourself to the Lord, and He will
help you remember the time when you first fell in
love with Jesus.

For reflection:

1. Do you need to restore the joy of your salvation?
Do you need to rekindle your passion for the things
of the Lord? Read the first fifteen verses of Psalm
51 and reflect:

• Are there unconfessed sins that you need to
bring to the Lord so that you can open your lips
and sing of His praises? If so, take the time now
to lay them at the altar. He is able to restore your
joy if you let Him.

• Do you still have your joy? Yes? How have you maintained it? If not, how do you hope to recover it? Whatever your response, please record your answers in a journal or on your phone. One day, you will need a reminder either for yourself or someone else that "the shout of joy comes in the morning."

Chapter Three

Too many Christians are no longer fishers of men but keepers of the aquarium.

—Paul Harvey

LIVING THE GOSPEL:
THE FOCUS AND INTENTIONALITY
OF THE COMMITTED
CHRISTIAN LIFE

Imitate me, just as I also imitate Christ.
(1 Corinthians 11:1)

But imitate those who through faith and
patience inherit the promises.
(Hebrews 6:12)

If I were to wager a bet, I'd bet that most of you were not saved at one of those big tent events. You did not get saved listening to Billy Graham, Luis Palau, Joseph Prince, or T. D. Jakes. Not that it does not happen—it is just not the way that most of us come to the Lord. For most of us, our witnessing of the life of someone close to us inspired the path to salvation—someone we respected and maybe even loved.

Maybe it was a parent or grandparent or a close friend. Perhaps it was a coworker or classmate. For most of us, there was somebody in our lives that lived life in a manner that was distinct from other people. They did not respond to the vicissitudes of life like others. When others got angry and bitter and cursed people out, they smiled and maintained a sunny disposition. When they ran into a rough patch of life where others would have given up, they kept pushing on. Come what may, they did not acquiesce to the tumult of the emotions of the moment. They responded differently. They did not ignore wrong—they just moved past it, never allowing themselves to get knocked off their square.

And when we faced trials in our lives, we wanted to summon that same equanimity, that same balance, that same inner strength. We were not familiar with the phrase yet, but we saw peace that surpassed all understanding, and quietly, we were in awe. It was these people, living lives that reflected something profoundly different, that we recalled when we seriously began to consider Christ. Their example and their model made all the difference.

When I was a young boy, there was nobody I wanted to be like more than my father. When others looked to movie stars or athletes as exemplars of who they would like to be, I was mesmerized by George Everest Alexander Providence Sr. He had what today we would call "swag," a way of being that I found incredibly appealing. At school, I remember being asked who my hero was—whom I most wanted to be like—and I said without hesitation that I wanted to be like my father when I grew up. It was his life—or more accurately, his way of being—that I wanted to imitate.

There is something profoundly personal about the practice of imitation, for it is an expression of a desire to be something different, to be something more. In imitation, we are seeking transformation. We are trying to elevate from where we are to somewhere better.

There are eyes on you, my brother, my sister, whether you want them there or not. People are looking at you, evaluating you. They are lining up your walk with your profession of faith and coming to some conclusions about the efficacy of Jesus. More than what you say, they are looking at what you do. Many of us—too many of us—get caught up trying to find the right thing to say. We want to know the trick, the technique, the secret code of evangelism that, once learned, will turn a sinner into a saint when, in actuality, it is more than what we say. The truism is in fact true: actions speak louder than words.

This is not to say that what you say is of no significance. It is. It is just that what you say can never be divorced from what you do—how you live. Your "conversation" is of marked importance. By *conversation*, I am referencing the King James Version use of the word. Today, when we use the word *conversation*, we think of discussion, talking, the exchange of ideas, communicated through speaking, one to another. But, for those of us who still have a KJV in our library, *conversation* has a more expanded meaning. In Galatians 1:13 (KJV), when Paul says that "ye have heard of my conversation," he is not referencing what the Galatians may have heard him say. He is talking about his way of life, or in this instance, his former way of life. Similarly, in Ephesians 4:22 (KJV), when Paul says, "Ye put off concerning the former conversation the old man, which is corrupt according to the deceitful lusts," he is speaking of lifestyle, not speech. Your conversation in this sense is both what you say and how you live.

Similarly, when I talk about the presentation of the Gospel, I do not limit that presentation to words alone. Indeed, the most authentic and best representation of the Gospel of Christ is how you live it—how you model the joy, freedom, and abandonment of the values of this world and freely embrace the rule of Jesus in your life and in your heart.

Are you looking for something better in your Christian walk? Do you want more of Him, more of Christ? Follow Him. Imitate Him. If you genuinely seek to fulfill the mission of Christ to preach the Gospel and to make disciples, you will start by imitating Christ.

You have heard it said that imitation is the sincerest form of flattery. When we do as we have seen others do, there is an implicit affirmation of that which is being imitated. We are, as it were, praising the thing we are imitating. In addition, we are doing something more. We are assigning value and worth to that which is being imitated. We are saying through our imitation that the object of our imitation is worthy of the act of imitation. An earlier iteration of the "imitation-is-flattery" proverb is found in a biography of Marcus Aurelius, who said: "You should consider that Imitation is the most acceptable part of Worship, and that the

Gods had much rather Mankind should Resemble, than Flatter them."[1] Now, for Christians, there is no plurality of gods, just the One, but the sentiment here is what I am getting at. The imitation, emulation, and replication of Jesus Christ is our sincerest form of both praise and worship, and if we would honor the mission of Christ to save souls, then this is our pursuit. When a commentator says of Paul that not only did he tell others how they should live, but he also lived the life he advocated, he is making concrete the inextricable link between word and deed. Paul's conversation exampled a life dedicated to Christ and as such is a blueprint for others to follow. This is an important point, for I fear that too many of us are looking for people to "get saved" without giving them any evidence that getting saved will lead to something different. "Do as I say and not as I do" has never worked—ask any parent. We must live the redeemed life if we are going to preach the redeeming Word. We must show others a credible demonstration that who the Lord has set free is free indeed. That credible demonstration—that proof positive that the blood

---

1. Marcus Aurelius, *The Emperor Marcus Antoninus: His Conversation with Himself*, trans. Jeremy Collier (London: Richard Sare, 1701), 186.

of Christ is efficacious to create new life—*is you*. You have probably heard it said that the only Bible that many people—maybe even most—will ever read is you. You are a living testimony—a walking witness to the goodness of life in Christ. You are the model that others can look at to see how to live in and for Christ.

My father had the distinction of being the first black bricklayer in the city of New Haven, Connecticut. He took pride in the achievement but also in the skill level that he achieved on the job. He was a meticulous craftsman and a student of the craft of masonry. Two of my brothers followed him into the trade, and he did his best to teach them. His instruction was always in two parts. He would tell them what to do, and then he would say to them to watch him and imitate. This should be instructive for each one of us. To evangelize—to accomplish the mission of Jesus—we must become experts in the living of the Gospel and be willing to instruct others in the way that they, too, should live. James Brown told the world to "watch me; I got it.... I got something that makes me wanna shout; I got something that tells me what it's all about."[2]

---

2. James Brown, "Super Bad," 1970, from *Super Bad*, Starday-King Studios, Nashville.

We, too, must be at least this bold.

For reflection:

1. There are eyes on you. Though you know that there are folks who observe you from afar, what of the people that you see every day? Make a list of the people in your life who are most impacted by your "conversation." Limit the list to ten names.

2. As you think of those names, what would each individual need to see in you to help them become more receptive to the message of the Gospel?

3. Select one of the names. If you had to share with that person the Gospel according to you—what Jesus's life has meant to you—what would it be?

4. Now, this is a big one: ask the Lord for His guidance and look for an opportunity to share the Gospel with that special someone. Our Lord will do the rest.

Chapter Four

I would sooner bring one sinner to Jesus Christ than unravel all of the mysteries of the divine Word, for salvation is the one thing we are to live for.

—Charles Haddon Spurgeon

DIGGING DEEP:
RECALLING THE REASON WHY

I beseech you therefore, brethren, by the
mercies of God, that you present your
bodies a living sacrifice, holy, acceptable
to God, which is your reasonable service.
And do not be conformed to this world,
but be transformed by the renewing of
your mind, that you may prove what is
that good and acceptable and perfect will
of God. (Romans 12:1–2)

I sat in the bleachers of the old elementary-school
gymnasium, the seats crowded with parents,
grandparents, and kids of all ages and relations,
and listened to them roar with a robust mixture
of cheers and howls as my elder daughter com-
pleted a three-play sequence (three-pointer, steal
and assist, coast-to-coast layup) that turned the tide

of the game in favor of her team and announced her arrival as a player to be reckoned with. The opposing coach rushed to call a timeout for his suddenly flustered team, and as my daughter headed toward her team's bench, I watched her smile as her jubilant teammates swarmed her. As the crowd noise subsided to an audible hum, I remembered. I remembered my parents sitting in the stands when I was a boy playing football, soaking in the cheers for their eldest child.

Sitting in that gym watching my elder daughter on the court and feeling the presence of my younger daughter beside me, I thought of the tremendous effort it had taken my parents to raise me and my five brothers. There were hard choices they often made so that we might have, even if that meant that they must deny themselves something they wanted. They struggled for us, fought for us, and poured themselves out for us. They did both realize professional and personal successes, yes, but as I sat in the bleachers, what I remembered the most were the hardships and humiliations they each endured so that their children might have. I realized at that moment in that old gymnasium that I loved my parents more deeply than I had ever known, because I then understood what my parents had truly done with their lives. Day by day, month to month, year after year, my parents gave their lives over and spent the substance of their earthly existence for the betterment of their sons—for the betterment of me. They sacrificed, and that sacrifice, now crystallized, engendered within me a desire to reciprocate—to sacrifice for those that loved me first.

Maybe you feel that same way about your parents, yes? Well, if so, riddle me this: if our earthly parents can provoke such a desire in you and me, how much more stoked should we be by the sacrifice of our Heavenly Father? What level of sacrifice are we willing to give in exchange for all that He has done on our behalf? We would give everything, right?

Of course, we would all answer yes. I know we would—or at least we would have, back in the day. Back when we were yet astonished at the sheer audacity of our salvation, that the Son of Man deigned to give His life so that we might escape the shackles of a sin-filled life, we would have given Him all that we had. Back when we marveled at the miracle of forgiveness and that His death on the cross paid our sin debt in full, we held nothing back. Yes, back in the day, we would have forfeited all to honor Jesus, the Christ. We talked to Him the first thing in the morning. We consorted with Him throughout the day. At night, we quieted ourselves so that we could hear the low whisper of His voice before we closed our eyes to sleep. He was our first and last, our be-all and end-all, and we denied Him nothing.

But now? Now, many of us—far too many of us, if we are honest in the moment—would give a much more muted, measured response. We have allowed the demands of life and the inclinations of our still-corrupted flesh to rob us of our desire to please Jesus. Living life sacrificially is a concept in vile opposition to most of our chosen lifestyles. Many of our choices are fueled by worldly aspirations, thoughts, and actions that are anathema to a transformed life. To the extent that this is true, we live as did those whom Paul referenced in Philippians 2:21—so busy getting ours that we do not seek the things of Christ. Indeed, we often work at cross-purposes to the Petrine assertion that "he who has suffered in the flesh has ceased from sin, that he no longer should live the rest of his time in the flesh for the lusts of men, but for the will of God" (1 Peter 4:1-2). And, in the eyes of the unbelieving world—that world that we are commissioned to save—we come up short. Alas, we are too much like them.

No, they do not know Christ, but intuitively, they understand that when they look at us, they should not see themselves. They do not know Christ, but they do know that He gave His all—His life for others—and they expect that we, as followers of Christ, would do the same. Except we do not. As they examine our lives to see if there is reconciliation between word and deed (if ever we are bold enough to publicly claim fidelity to Christ), they see more of themselves than they do Jesus. At work, at school, at the gym, in the stores, on the roads, at home, or even—Lord forgive us—at church, we speak as they speak, react as they react, and do as they do. We might indeed proclaim the Gospel with our lips, but the unsaved look at our day-to-day living and determine that it is much ado about nothing. Why? Our unwillingness to give our all for Him—our reticence to live sold out to Him and His mission—eviscerates the message of the preached Gospel, and not because the good news of Jesus Christ has no agency. The message of the good news is evacuated of its power because we do not value it enough to sacrifice ourselves for it.

Leaf through the pages of any dictionary to the entry for the word *sacrifice*, or search the internet for a definition of the same, and you will find that it is defined as "the surrender or destruction of something prized or desirable." Why would one do this, you might ask? "For the sake of something considered as having a higher or more pressing claim."[1] The one sacrificing, in effect, exchanges that which is presently valued for something that is believed to be of more value. Think about that for a moment. Let it marinate and settle in your spirit. To sacrifice is to let go of that which is possessed in pursuit of something greater—something higher. Can you see the resonance of this definition of *sacrifice* with the life of Christ and with the expectation of the life of a follower of Christ—the expectation for you and me?

There is, however, another understanding of sacrifice, also found in most dictionaries. Read just a little further down and you will see that *sacrifice* is further defined as "a loss incurred in selling something below its value." This understanding of sacrifice indicates that the thing given is knowingly exchanged for something of lower value. At first blush, this is not in and of itself a bad thing.

---

1. *WordReference Random House Unabridged Dictionary of American English*, s.v. "sacrifice (*n.*)," accessed January 30, 2024, wordreference.com/definition/sacrifice.

One donates something of value to a charity or an individual knowing this, or at least not expecting anything in return. Indeed, that might be the express purpose of the gift—to bless someone else without burdening them with the expectation or responsibility of giving something in return.

But this second understanding of sacrifice is problematic when within our hearts we give grudgingly or out of a sense of obligation. A person so possessed gives but feels put upon and, in a sense, is resentful and measures the costs and benefits in the exchange. Having performed the necessary calculations, said person usually determines that what is to be received in return for the sacrifice is of little value and proceeds to calibrate the giving or gift to the diminished expectations. This person gives less because he does not value what he expects to come back to him. Giving in this manner is not sacrificial; it is transactional. He provides only that which is required to satisfy.

Here I wonder about the way in which many of our churches of today go about the business of soliciting monies from their members, but that is a conversation for another time—the point being that, too frequently, we give for appearances' sake. And when we give in this manner, we diminish and disdain what we give and—most damningly—what we have received.

Unfortunately for the church of today that is "a mile wide but an inch deep," this last understanding of sacrifice seems to reflect how we treat the Christian life. Because we no longer remember the time when He was the beginning and end of our existence—no longer recall how blessed we were to receive the gift of everlasting life—we now give only that portion of ourselves that we determine will not interrupt our chosen way of life. We give because He will open up the floodgates and pour out riches, He will move us from the back to the front, from the bottom to the top (won't He do it?). He will get us into our rightful place at the head, not the tail. The cold, unvarnished truth is that for many of us, we give and sacrifice not because of what He has done for us but because of what He can do for us. Yes, we "sacrifice," but there is no life, no revelation, and no power in this kind of sacrifice because we have forgotten the object and the objective of our sacrifice. We have forgotten that we are sacrificing for Him.

Sacrifice—true Christian sacrifice—is what Paul is pleading for in the first two verses of Romans chapter 12. To help the Roman believers get their minds right, Paul reminds them in the last verse of chapter 11 that all things are of God, all things are through God, and all things are to God and that He is to receive glory ad infinitum. Because of this truth, Roman believers—and by extension, believers of today—must surrender themselves as living sacrifices.

Why does Paul believe that this is our "reasonable service"? Because he knows that we are surrendering a prize of estimable value for one of inestimable value. We give our lives so that others might receive what we now cherish—life in the bosom of Christ, a life blessed in all things, regardless of the situation or the circumstance. We are living sacrifices—the emphasis on "living." We are challenged to "live" for Him. Why? Because as we are transformed and that transformation is reflected in our lives, we will become proof positive of "that good and acceptable and perfect will of God." And that proof is what we are to provide for a disbelieving world. Yes, you, my sister, and yes, you, my brother—your life and your choices as guided by a renewed mind are the living proof of the power, the mercy, and the love of Jesus.

Later in chapter 12, Paul paints a picture of what a sacrificial, transformed life looks like. Among other things, it is a life where persecution for His sake is met by blessing, not cursing, and where we Christians empathize with those around us, whether they be in joy or pain. Humility is ever present, and we live in peace with all. There is much prayer in this life—much hope—and trial and suffering are endured gracefully. The man or woman changed by their embrace of Christ will love sincerely and have nothing to do with evil. They will be proactive in seeking to meet the needs of those who, like them, have been transformed, and—most provocatively—these people will feed their enemies. Can you imagine the impact of this kind of life on those who are in its orbit? I know you can, because most of you—most of us—saw living sacrifices, and it was these living sacrifices we referenced in authenticating the efficacy of the Gospel for ourselves. It is this life of sacrifice that is missing from the life of the Church and the life of today's Christian. A life that is genuinely sacrificed to God will powerfully affect the lives of the world and powerfully impact those around us—our family, friends, colleagues, and even those who might call us foe.

Remember, you were once lost but now have been redeemed "of Him and through Him and to Him," so give to Him all that is precious to you—your very being. Surrender yourself. Do this because you have faith in what you will receive in exchange for what you give, your confidence bolstered because of what you have already received from God. It is only in this surrender—this total surrender—that we are pleasing to God and we are that sweet aroma.

Finally, it is as simple, as stark, and as plain as your answer to this query: Are you indeed clay in the hands of the Potter—the tool that is fit for His use—or are you more akin to those in the world? Those who have surrendered themselves to God with abandon are able to soldier through the dark moments of life with assurance that they are in God's hands and being used for His purposes. Those more akin to the world are like those who value above all else that which they want for themselves. They are not unlike that fallen angel who, dissatisfied with the role he played in creation, wanted more and forever doomed himself and all who follow his path. My deepest prayer is that you answer rightly, for yourself and for those that you impact. Your Heavenly Father emptied Himself for you. You, in turn, are called to do no less for Him.

I submit to you, my brother, my sister, that we cannot live this way if we live without completely pouring ourselves out into the transformation of our minds and our lives. We cannot continue to walk in the ways of this world, caught so obviously under the sway of the fallen one. Instead, we must walk in the way of our Savior, with a tenacity and intentionality that is rooted in a deep-seated desire to honor our Father and make Him proud.

For reflection:

1. What does Jesus's sacrifice mean to you?

2. How do you see His sacrifice reflected in your life?

3. What would your life look like if Jesus were the centerpiece of your existence?

Chapter Five

We are too busy to pray, and so we have no power. We have a great deal of activity, but we accomplish little; many services but few conversions; much machinery but few results.

—R. A. Torrey

ENTER THE RIVER

Here are some final thoughts. There are three elements of the Gospel message, or the good news, and here I echo the views of the theologian Walter Brueggemann from his book *Biblical Perspectives on Evangelism: Living in a Three-Storied Universe*.[1] First, there is the victory that has been won in the war of God versus the enemy. This victory has occurred in a space and time that we who yet live have not witnessed and have not participated in.

We know of this victory because it has been proclaimed to us by others. It is this proclamation—this report—that is the second part of the Gospel. We have been told that the enemy has been defeated and we are now free from his bondage.

---

1. Walter Brueggemann, *Biblical Perspectives on Evangelism: Living in a Three-Storied Universe* (Nashville: Abingdon, 1993).

Unless we receive that news, we are enslaved to the old world order, much like the American slaves who did not hear the news of the victory of the North over the South until two years after the fact. Far from the battlefield and oblivious to the new reality, these free black men and black women lived as if the victory were still in question and as if there were still the possibility of defeat. It was not until the news of victory reached their ears that they were able to celebrate the new life. With the knowledge of victory came freedom and the opportunity for life as a free people.

And it is this fact that brings our freedom as well. There is a new reality for us in the last part of the Gospel message—its apprehension, our appropriation—our ownership, if you will—of that received good news, and our willingness to live anew in the new reality.

Relationship is the key to evangelism. It is out of our relationship with Jesus Christ that evangelism and our engagement with it are inspired. It is our relationship with others that affords us the opportunity to proclaim the good news. Brueggemann says, "Because God lives in stories that permit a gamut of experience from fear, affront, and dismay to joy, surprise, and delight, it is clear that God lives on the lips of story-tellers."[2] I agree with him. Evangel is the good news—the good news that we were lost but now are found—were blind, but now we see. Though we were born in sin and destined for hell, destined for the perpetual torture of inextinguishable torment and pain, Jesus Christ called us and saved us. The good news is that His arms are strong enough to lift us from the pit of despair and settle us amongst the clouds of joy. The good news is that we can stand before the Most High, unabashed and unafraid and fearless, for Christ died on our behalf. He intercedes for us. He stands between us and the punishment that we deserve.

This relationship reminds me of the dynamic in my home when I was growing up. I am the eldest of six sons (that's right, no girls!), and as is to be expected, we would occasionally get caught up in mess, and sometimes that mess was a punishable offense. We fell under the terrible wrath of our father. It was not a wrath that visited us unprovoked. No, it was a wrath that sought to deal with a transgression of the rules of the house as clearly and patiently dictated by my parents. We did wrong,

---

2. Brueggemann, *Biblical Perspectives on Evangelism*, 113.

and we would be—justifiably so given the dictates previously established—punished for our misdeeds. And the wrath would descend at the appointed time—except on those blessed occasions when our mother would stand as a buffer between our father and us. She would mediate on our behalf and shield us from the deserved punishment, absorbing within her psyche that which was meant for us. In return for that mediation—that intercession—in return for her love for us and our father, her husband, we all loved and still love her.

As a demonstration of our appreciation for her standing in the gap, we sought out ways to show her our love. If this is true due to the act of a mother on behalf of both her sons and their father, how much more is it so for the act of our Savior, standing before the Heavenly Father and bearing the wrath that must fall so that we might live? As my mother loved my father and his children, so does Jesus love His Father and His children, and it is out of love—a deep, abiding, never-ebbing love—that Jesus acted to save you and me. It is this love, manifest in a fully surrendered life, that will save those that we love and those that we are in relationship with.

For reflection:

Though it may seem hard to believe, getting people to show up at the church is easy. The question is, what are we going to do with them once they get here?

1. Is your church prepared to be a witness in the post-Christian world? If so, how? If not, why not?

2. Does your church engage the secular seeker or the secular/spiritual seeker? Both? How?

3. Rate your congregation on the following, using a scale of 1–5, with 5 representing the best and 1 representing the worst:

  • We are open and accessible to others. _____
  • We preach the exclusive message of Christ victorious. _____
  • We create a sense of community for all. _____

4. Do you reach out into the broader social network of the church

  • Through neighborhood groups?
  • In believers' homes?
  • By eating together?

For evaluation:

• Does your church embody the faith in your community?

• Are new converts and newcomers immersed in the reality of the community of your congregation? Are they immersed in the reality of the community at large?

Epilogue

When I was in full-time ministry, responsible for developing strategies for outreach and evangelism and finding ways to bridge the divide between those who were on the inside of the church and those who were on the outside, I was frequently confronted with doubts about the possibility of change. *You have great ideas, George, and a lot of heart, but things just will not change.* This was a source of frustration for me, and in my darker moments, I would become dour. How could I seek to do this work when so few believed that change was possible? But one day, as I was listening to a radio program, "Truth that Transforms," I heard Dr. D. James Kennedy of Coral Ridge Ministries and Evangelism Explosion recite a poem that totally changed my perspective. This is it in its entirety:

I Wanted to Change the World

When I was a young man, I wanted to change the world.

I found it was difficult to change the world, so I tried to change my nation.

When I found I couldn't change the nation, I began to focus on my town. I couldn't change the town, and as an older man, I tried to change my family.

Now, as an old man, I realize the only thing I can change is myself, and suddenly I realize that if long ago I had changed myself, I could have made an impact on my family. My family and I could have made an impact on our town. Their impact could have changed the nation, and I could indeed have changed the world.[1]

Similarly, Robert Coleman says, "One cannot transform a world except as individuals in the world are transformed, and individuals cannot be

---

1. Source unknown. Attributed online to Unknown Monk, approx. AD 1200.

changed except as they are molded in the hands of the Master."[2]

Now when people doubt that change can occur, I tell them I can guarantee change because I will change. Change has occurred and is happening in me.

Will you, my brother, my sister, guarantee the same? You can change the world for Christ. Jesus has already shown you the way.

---

2. Robert E. Coleman, *The Master Plan of Evangelism* (Grand Rapids: Revell, 1993), 24.